Notes to self...

Notes to self...

Notes to self...

Notes to self...

Notes to self...

Notes to self...

Notes to self...

Notes to self...

Notes to self...

Notes to self...

Notes to self...

Notes to self...

Notes to self...

Notes to self...

Notes to self...

Notes to self...

Notes to self...

Notes to self...

Notes to self...

Notes to self...

Notes to self...

Notes to self...

Notes to self...

Notes to self...

Notes to self...

Notes to self...

Notes to self...

Notes to self...

Notes to self...

Notes to self...

Notes to self...

Notes to self...

Notes to self...

Notes to self...

Notes to self...

Notes to self...

Notes to self...

Notes to self...

Notes to self...

Notes to self...

Notes to self...

Notes to self...

Notes to self...

Notes to self...

Notes to self...

Notes to self...

Notes to self...

Notes to self...

Notes to self...

Notes to self...

Notes to self...

Notes to self...

Notes to self...

Notes to self...

Notes to self...

Notes to self...

Notes to self...

Notes to self...

Notes to self...

Notes to self...

Notes to self...

Notes to self...

Notes to self...

Notes to self...

Notes to self...

Notes to self...

Notes to self...

Notes to self...

Notes to self...

Notes to self...

Notes to self...

Notes to self...

Notes to self...

Notes to self...

Notes to self...

Notes to self...

Notes to self...

Notes to self...

Notes to self...

Notes to self...

Notes to self...

Notes to self...

Notes to self...

Notes to self...

Notes to self...

Notes to self...

Notes to self...

Notes to self...

Notes to self...

Notes to self...

Notes to self...

Notes to self...

Notes to self...

Notes to self...

Notes to self...

Notes to self...

Notes to self...

Notes to self...

Notes to self...

Notes to self...